Living With
Schizophrenia

Living With Schizophrenia

A Brief Guide to Understanding and
Coping for Patients, Families, and Providers

Gregory S. Jurenec, PhD

To order additional copies of this book, contact:
Xlibris Corporation
1-888-795-4274
www.Xlibris.com
Orders@Xlibris.com
94067

CONTENTS

ACKNOWLEDGMENTS

First I need to acknowledge the many patients and families who enabled me to learn about their lives and so learn about their experience with schizophrenia. I also owe a debt of gratitude to Eleazar San Agustin, MD, who was so patient in repeatedly explaining to me the rationale behind psychotropic medications and the management of their side effects. I also owe thanks to Mary Stryck for her feedback on this manuscript. Lastly, I want to thank my wife, Anne, who has put up with the long and often unusual hours I have logged in private practice, on inpatient hospital wards, and teaching night classes. I am sure that she is relieved that I have finally finished this first book, and she will be expecting a second soon.

INTRODUCTION

My interest in schizophrenia probably began in my teens, along with my interest in psychology. Both were a consequence of my mother's influence. She told me stories about her work as an aide at the Milwaukee County Asylum (yes, that's what it was called then) when she was in college. This was before the discovery of antipsychotic medications, so people who were severely ill had to be isolated in cells and sometimes restrained. She was also an avid student of the famous Swiss psychologist Carl Jung. His theories focused on the symbolism and meaning of dreams, fantasies, art, and mythology. This seemed to indicate that the hallucinations of schizophrenia could be a window to the unconscious mind. In fact, Carl Jung was very interested in schizophrenia and worked a great deal with patients hospitalized with this condition (again, long before the discovery of medication). My first *formal* introduction to schizophrenia began in the late 1970s when I entered graduate school to become a clinical psychologist. I studied under two professors who were very interested in doing therapy with persons who had mild schizophrenia and had published papers on the topic. These professors sparked my interest, and I joined their schizophrenia research group. My first contact with people suffering from schizophrenia came during my internship in clinical psychology at Baylor College of Medicine, in Houston, Texas. I was fascinated with what my patients told me about their experiences of the schizophrenic condition, particularly their hallucinations, delusions, and their efforts to cope and make sense out of them. Since I was one of the few people who took the time to listen, they were often eager to tell me about their psychotic experiences. As they told me about their struggles to cope with and understand their illness, I began to appreciate the impact these symptoms must have on a person's life.

In the course of my years of training and practice, I have probably worked with a couple thousand persons suffering from schizophrenia in outpatient clinics, day programs, acute hospital settings, and long-term rehabilitation settings. As a result, I have been able to learn a great deal from my patients as well as their families and the social workers, case managers, nurses, and psychiatrists with whom I worked. I have found that one of the most helpful things I can do for a patient or family is to pass on to them what I have learned about schizophrenia—that is, help them understand their schizophrenia. Over the years, I have spent countless hours providing explanations of symptoms and causes of schizophrenia, debunking misinformation, and giving tips on coping. It finally dawned on me that I might be able to share this information more effectively if I wrote it down in a practical format for patients and families. My first drafts were well received by patients and families. To my pleasant surprise, many of the hospital treatment staff also found the material in my early drafts of this book to be useful in supplementing their appreciation and understanding of schizophrenia. They also found it to be very helpful in the psychoeducational groups they ran on the hospital ward. Now that I have theoretically retired from clinical practice to teach at a university, I have continued to revise and update what I started, leading to the current product. However, even though it is technically "finished," it will always be a work in progress as I myself learn more about schizophrenia. I expect there will be more revisions in the future.

As the title indicates, this material is intended for the use of patients, families, and providers in order for them to better understand and manage the problems associated with schizophrenia. I am always interested in adding ideas, insights, and strategies that people have found helpful. I would welcome your ideas and comments. I can be contacted by e-mail or mail:

Gregory Jurenec, PhD
Wisconsin School of Professional Psychology
9120 West Hampton Avenue
Milwaukee, Wisconsin 53225-4960
gjurenec@wspp.edu

WHAT IS SCHIZOPHRENIA?

Schizophrenia is a chronic illness that affects the way the brain works. As a result, this illness causes problems with thinking, perception, and emotions. "Chronic" means that it is a lifelong illness: once it starts, you have it for the rest of your life. The condition usually starts in the late teens or early twenties, but sometimes earlier. For instance, someone in their early teens may begin to have trouble with concentration because of unwanted thoughts coming into their head, or they may show mild confusion and unusual thinking. These kinds of problems may then progress to very peculiar thinking that gets in the way of functioning or to auditory hallucinations (hearing things others do not hear). Their ability to cope with worsening symptoms can eventually lead to a breakdown that *everyone* notices. Most of the time, the symptoms (or problems the illness causes) can be controlled with treatment, to a greater or lesser extent. The degree to which the symptoms can be controlled varies from a little bit to almost completely. The severity of the disorder also varies enormously. A few people become so severely ill that they need to stay in a hospital or a supervised living arrangement for most of their life. At the other extreme, some people become ill only when under particular stress and then recover completely. These people may not even be *formally* diagnosed with schizophrenia. Instead, it may be called brief psychotic disorder or schizotypal personality disorder. This range of disorders, from mild to severe, are sometimes called *schizophrenia spectrum disorders*.

Schizophrenia affects the way that the brain processes, interprets, and acts upon information. That means schizophrenia affects how a person perceives, thinks, and feels. Let me explain these problems a little bit, one at a time.

Perceiving refers to what a person hears, sees, or the way they interpret events (what they believe is going on). In schizophrenia, this perception may not match reality. For instance, I may hear voices or sounds that are not actually there. Or I may see two people talking and laughing and conclude that they are making fun of me, when in fact their conversation has nothing to do with me. Or I may believe terrorists are spying on me through the television, which obviously is impossible.

By "thinking," I mean the *way* a person reasons or their *process* of thinking. Often, a person's logic becomes mixed up and confused when they have schizophrenia. Their thinking is sometimes called "tangential," meaning that they may jump from one topic to another without any connection between the two. Sometimes their logic does not make sense. For instance, a person with schizophrenia might reason something like this: because you scratched your left leg, it means that you are going to tell a lie or that you are working for the FBI.

Lastly, emotions are often affected. Sometimes this is simply a lack of feeling, like a lack of concern about anything. On the other hand, the patient may have emotions, but they are indistinct or fuzzy. One of my patients described it as like a TV without any fine-tuning. In other cases, the emotions don't match what is going on: I might be laughing about something sad, become angry about a joke, or become very sad for no reason.

Because our thoughts, perceptions, and emotions determine our actions, these symptoms of schizophrenia will influence the way a person behaves. However, it is important to emphasize that *schizophrenia does not affect everyone in exactly the same way*.

This means that different people with schizophrenia will often behave quite differently from one another, even though they may have the same *symptoms*. Two people may be very paranoid and suspicious yet react in very different ways: one may become aggressive and violent as a way to protect himself from a perceived threat, while another may withdraw, isolate in his room, and become depressed and anxious.

Furthermore, people with schizophrenia can have different *combinations* of symptoms. Some people may hear "voices," while some become very paranoid and others very confused. If you consider some of the familiar things that affect the brain's function, this makes perfect sense. For example, alcohol intoxication is due to a temporary effect of alcohol on the brain. The neurochemical effect of alcohol is fundamentally the same for everyone who drinks it. However, as is common knowledge, there are great differences between people when they are intoxicated: some are relaxed and social, some are very aggressive, while others become depressed and even suicidal. In addition, the *same* person may respond *differently* to alcohol on *different* occasions.

Therefore, not everyone who has schizophrenia will have the same symptoms, the same severity of symptoms, or the same reaction to the symptoms. Here are some of the reasons for these differences:

- Some people accept the fact that they have schizophrenia and then work hard to understand and manage it. Others exert all of their energy to *deny* to themselves and others that they are ill, thus avoiding treatment and allowing the illness to take over their lives.
- Some people make the symptoms worse by using street drugs like marijuana, cocaine, or crack.
- The expression of schizophrenia, or the way a person actually behaves, can be greatly affected by a person's experiences and personality. For instance, if a person has been taught that having a mental illness is a sign of weakness, they might be afraid to get help. Others may have been told that their hallucinations and delusions are spiritual issues, possibly a consequence of some sin they believe they have committed. Therefore, they may believe that they can only be helped by faith and prayer. Unfortunately, this point of view can lead to guilt and shame when the patient fails to improve, because they may believe that their problems continue because they are a bad person.
- As is discussed in a later section, schizophrenia is most likely a genetic disorder and is passed on through the parents' genes. There are probably many genes that contribute to schizophrenia. Therefore, the number and combination of genes inherited may be a large factor in the type and severity of symptoms.

As a result of these and other factors, the pattern of symptoms can be very different in different people. Different people who have schizophrenia may show different patterns of symptoms. Often, patients who are very paranoid, unable to concentrate, and are confused will argue that they do not have schizophrenia because they do not hallucinate. Some people have severe hallucinations, but have never been paranoid. Others have only severe confusion, act in ways that are embarrassing to others, and show emotions that do not fit the situation. Nonetheless, all of these patients suffer from the same fundamental disorder. Below, the most common symptoms seen in schizophrenia will be described. A patient may have only a few of these symptoms, or they may have nearly all of them. Similarly, any of these problems could be very mild or severe or anywhere in between. Just to make things complicated, I have found that the pattern of symptoms can *change* over time. For example, I may first see a young man who feels very paranoid and angry because he is convinced that people are spying on him, although he hears no voices. Several years later, when he is readmitted to the hospital, he may have very different symptoms. At this time he may be suicidal because of the voices he hears that are telling him that he is worthless and that he should kill himself.

The Major Symptoms of Schizophrenia

Symptoms are the observable signs of a disorder or condition. For instance, a prominent sign or symptom of mumps is that the lymph nodes in the neck are swollen, producing visible lumps. Chicken pox is characterized by a fever and little bumps or rash on the skin. The idea is that these symptoms are an indication of an underlying illness that produces these symptoms. If you have read this far, you will have noticed that I have been writing about some of these symptoms for schizophrenia, such as hallucinations.

Hallucinations. These are sensory perceptions (like hearing and seeing something) that are not actually real. The most common hallucinations are auditory: the person may hear voices, sounds, or music that no one else hears. The voices heard may be friendly, give advice, or make jokes. Often, however, they are threatening, mean, and critical. Sometimes the voices "command" the person to do things. These commands may even include self-harm or assaulting others. Voices may "inform" the person that others are making fun of them or are planning to harm them. Sometimes people identify these voices as belonging to God, Jesus, or the devil. This experience can be very frightening. For some people, these "voices" can seem more like they are "inside their head," kind of like loud, intrusive thoughts that are not their own. Less often, people with schizophrenia have *visual hallucinations*. That is, they *see* people or things that are not really there. Occasionally, people report tactile hallucinations. This is the feeling that something or someone is touching you when in fact there is nothing there. Rarely, patients claim to taste or smell things that are not there. These last two types, which are called "gustatory" and "olfactory" hallucinations, may indicate that the person is suffering from a neurological condition *other* than schizophrenia.

Delusions. These are beliefs or interpretations that are obviously untrue. However, the person is not lying or "making things up." The experience seems absolutely real to the person suffering from the delusion. Sometimes delusions can be about identity: the patient may believe he is God, a famous musician, an agent for the FBI, or that he is secretly married to Princess Diana, who is not really dead. Sometimes they are *grandiose*—that is, they reflect an exaggeration of self-importance. Patients have told me that they were Jesus, the president of the United States, the chief justice of the Supreme Court, and so on. Others told me of impossible powers, riches, or skills they had. Delusions can be *persecutory*, the belief that they are being harmed in some way. Patients have told me they feared they were being poisoned, plotted against, lied about, or being tortured and raped in their sleep. These delusions can become more complicated, involving plots and conspiracies. Anyone who does not believe the person may then be seen as an enemy and *part* of the conspiracy against them. Further, no amount of reasoning can convince the person their delusion is untrue. One lady had the delusion that she was shrinking. To try to dissuade her, the psychologist (a friend of mine) marked her height on the wall daily. After a week, he showed her the marks on the wall, which were all at the same height. Her interpretation was, "The building is shrinking too." In another case, a woman drove her car onto to a military base and insisted on speaking with the commanding officer. She claimed that she had received satellite transmissions from the president, and she refused to leave until she could communicate these to the commanding officer. The military personnel were very concerned that she could be some kind of terrorist and had their guns pointed at her. Of course, this only added to her system of delusions. I have often heard patients claim that the CIA or FBI spied on them in order to steal some secret information. These beliefs continue to be held despite strong evidence they are wrong and despite advice of family, friends, and experts.

Paranoia. This can be simply unjustified suspiciousness or it can extend to complicated delusions. A person may have a delusion about being followed, persecuted, or sabotaged. For instance, the person may believe strangers are talking about them or laughing at them, plotting to harm them, stealing their thoughts, spying on them, and so on. Regarding paranoia and delusions, it is important to point out that a person's fears can sometimes be *true*, in which case seemingly irrational fears might *not* be a paranoid delusion. As an example, I saw one young man who covered all of the windows of his family's house with sheets. He would not leave the house or allow family members to answer the phone. He was terrified that people were looking for him and would kill him. It eventually emerged that he had been selling drugs for a gang, and he had spent a substantial amount of the drug money he was supposed to pay to the gang. Therefore, there *really were* people looking for him who had said they would kill him. In a very different situation, a young woman believed that she was being "blacklisted" by potential employers because she had broken off an affair with a former supervisor, who was now spreading false information to ruin her reputation. At first, this seemed quite possible, as members of her profession comprise a fairly interconnected community. However, it became clear this was a delusion when she also claimed that she could not go into a store or coffee shop because everyone would immediately recognize her and talk about her. She insisted that "lies" about her were constantly discussed on talk radio programs. The point here is that you should not be too quick to conclude that something is a delusion if it sounds odd or unlikely. Rather, it is important that you can see a general *pattern* of this kind of thinking before you decide the person is having delusions.

Ideas of reference. This is a particular type of delusion in which the individual believes that TV or radio programs, songs, stories, are actually about *them*. An example is the lady I discussed above who was sure that everyone knew about her situation because it was constantly discussed on all of the radio talk shows. Someone experiencing "ideas of reference" would assume that anyone they saw talking would be talking about them. They might also think popular songs, books, newspaper articles, and so on, were also somehow making "reference" to them or were about them.

Thought disorder. Thought processes can become confused, disorganized, or illogical. This is best illustrated by tasks of abstract reasoning, like interpreting proverbs. In some cases, people are inappropriately concrete and literal. For instance, I asked one patient to tell me what he thought the proverb "Don't count your chickens before they've hatched" meant. After careful thought, he became excited and asked, "I got chickens?"

In other cases, people make what are called "loose associations" to the topic, which means that they make connections that are not relevant. As an example, a person might respond in the following way to the proverb "Rome wasn't built in a day":

> The book Romans in the Bible is pretty long and probably took months to write. But I can roam on my cell phone, and that's pretty quick. It takes only a few seconds, not even a day. 'ET, phone home!' I love that movie! I believe aliens have been watching us for hundreds of years.

Emotions. Emotional functioning may not work like it does in everyone else. Sometimes the person may seem flat or emotionless. Or, the emotions shown by the person with schizophrenia may not fit the circumstances. They might giggle while talking about a sad event or becoming enraged over something very minor. More on this later.

Negative symptoms. The above symptoms, such as hallucinations and delusions, are often called "positive" symptoms. This isn't because they are good. It is because they are things that are *present* that you would prefer were *not* present. "Negative" symptoms refer to things that are *absent* that you would *like to be present*. For instance, sometimes a person with schizophrenia will seem very unmotivated. They may lie in bed or stay in their room all day. They may talk about getting a job, but still spend the entire day watching TV and smoking. It may seem like they can never "get started." So one common negative symptom is difficulty initiating action or getting started. Another negative symptom is often the lack of emotional expressiveness. This may seem like depression, but it is really just a kind of absence or bluntness of feelings. To the person with schizophrenia, everything can seem pretty much the same. Professionals call this "flat affect" ("affect" is another word for the expression of emotion). Related to this is a reduction in the ability to experience fun or pleasure, which is called "anhedonia." Often, people who have been ill for a long time are largely unable to really enjoy much of anything. Everything is kind of blah or neutral. This may be why people with long-term schizophrenia often get overly focused on the real basic "pleasures" like eating and smoking, which seem to become substitutes for enjoyment.

What Schizophrenia Is *Not*

There are many misconceptions about schizophrenia. These can present an enormous obstacle to a patient's acceptance of their illness. Here are a few of the common misconceptions:

- Schizophrenia is *not* "split personality." While a person may act differently when they are sick than when well, they do not have *different personalities* or different people inside of them. Imagine how you would act if you started to have symptoms of schizophrenia. For instance, what if you heard someone threatening or insulting you, but you could not see anyone? Wouldn't this experience make anyone act differently?

- Mental illness is *not* the same as mental retardation. If you have schizophrenia, it does not mean that you are stupid. Although people who have mental retardation *can* also have schizophrenia, there are also *brilliant* people who have schizophrenia as well. There is no connection between mental illness and intelligence. The movie *A Beautiful Mind* is one of the best depictions of schizophrenia I have seen, and it's a true story. While the main character is severely ill, he is still able to win the Nobel Prize in Economics! Similarly, in the movie/book *The Soloist*, the main character has severe symptoms of schizophrenia, but is a gifted musician.
- People with schizophrenia are not any more violent than the general population. When people with schizophrenia do become aggressive, it is most often because they feel scared or threatened.
- A diagnosis of schizophrenia does not mean you will be institutionalized all of your life or be turned into "a zombie" by medication. Of the people who develop schizophrenia, very few spend large parts of their lives in hospitals.
- People fear that they will be unable to do anything with their life if they have schizophrenia. They fear that they won't be able to work, have relationships, have a family, etc. In fact, if you take care of your illness, chances are good that you can have these things in your life, although you may have to work somewhat harder and longer than the next person. As an example, I attended a conference at which the main speaker was a nationally recognized psychologist who also had schizophrenia. She managed

her illness with medication and occasionally required brief hospitalizations. Nonetheless, she completed a doctorate in psychology, has written many professional articles, and gives lectures all over the country.

THE SPECTRUM OF
SCHIZOPHRENIA

A Note about Diagnosis

Diagnosis is a medical concept. The idea is to identify a cluster of observable "signs" that go together and can be linked to a particular cause. For instance, a fever and sore throat will lead your family doctor to take a swab from your throat and test to see if it contains certain bacteria. If it does, the doctor will prescribe an antibiotic. This will kill the bacteria causing the fever and sore throat. If you try to just lower your temperature and take medicine to numb your throat, you may feel better briefly; but since the underlying cause remains untreated, the fever and sore throat will keep coming back. Only the antibiotic will get at the *cause* of the problem. An attempt is made to apply the same idea to mental issues. A cluster of symptoms happening together is seen as defining a particular illness, which then helps determine how it is best treated. This idea works, more or less. If a person has many of the symptoms that define schizophrenia, it does tell us the type or class of medications that will probably help. However, it does not tell us which *specific* medication will work the best for a given person. Further, people are very complicated when it comes to emotions and behavior. Therefore, the exact diagnosis may change somewhat over time, depending on what symptoms are the worst at the time the person is seen.

There is another important note to make about diagnosis. I often hear professionals refer to their patients as "a schizophrenic." Similarly, many people I have worked with will refer to *themselves* as "a schizophrenic." It is very important to distinguish between a *diagnosis* and one's *identity*. For example, schizophrenia does not define who I am. Rather, I am a person with interests, skills, friends, a family, and hobbies—*who also has schizophrenia. Schizophrenia is not all that I am; it is just a part of who I am.*

Before we go further, it is necessary to give a short explanation of the "book of diagnosis" used by everyone in the mental health field. This book is the source of the diagnostic labels that I will be discussing.

The Diagnostic and Statistical Manual of Mental Disorders (Fourth Edition)

This is affectionately known as the DSM-IV, which is a lot easier to say. This is a comprehensive, highly detailed list and description of all of the currently recognized mental disorders. It is put together and published by the American Psychiatric Association. There are certainly problems with this system of classifying people, but that is a topic for another book.

Good or bad, this is the system of diagnosis that *everyone* uses today. This includes physicians, psychiatrists, nurses, social workers, psychologists, and so on. It is also used by insurance companies and government agencies in their decisions about what they will pay for and what they will not pay for. The DSM-IV generally separates mental health diagnoses into two very general types: clinical conditions and personality disorders. *Clinical conditions* are those clusters of problems or symptoms that are usually the reason someone is seeking help. Examples are schizophrenia—paranoid type, major depression, posttraumatic stress disorder, or anorexia. *Personality disorders* are a little different. These are long standing, even lifelong styles, attitudes, or perspectives we have about how we relate to the outside world. Rather than reflecting a particular problem, personality disorders reflect more of the kind of person someone is. To be a *disorder*, this particular style of relating has to be pretty extreme. Still, people rarely seek treatment for a personality disorder because they see this style of relating as *normal*; they have *always* been this way. But sometimes this personality style causes problems with relationships, employment, or school. This could include trouble keeping a relationship, repeated conflict with coworkers, or failing grades in school. The result of these problems can then lead to a *clinical condition* like depression. If this seems a little fuzzy, it's because it *is* a little fuzzy. There is certainly an overlap between the two kinds of diagnoses. I am mentioning it here because some of the milder conditions on the schizophrenia spectrum are considered to be personality disorders, rather than clinical conditions. However, as you will see in the descriptions to follow, these personality disorders seem to merge into clinical conditions. The personality disorders fall into three groups, or "clusters." The ones that are related to schizophrenia make up cluster A.

The Spectrum of Schizophrenia

There is actually a very broad range in the type and severity of the symptoms that people may have. Depending on the type and severity, a person may simply be a little unusual or eccentric, severely impaired and unable to function, or anything in between. Here are some of the diagnostic groups along the continuum. (See Figure 1.)

FIGURE 1
SPECTRUM OF SCHIZOPHRENIC DISORDERS

Cluster "A" Personality Disorders | Brief Psychotic Episode | Schizophreniform Disorder | Schizophrenias

SEVERITY OF SYMTOMS

Schizotypal Personality Disorder. This diagnosis falls on the mild end of the continuum. Such people seem to have odd thinking, although it doesn't quite meet the definition of "delusional." They want to have friends and fit in, but always seem to have trouble understanding people. Therefore, they are often embarrassed and ashamed of their blunders. There was a handsome, innocent young man I worked with who desperately wanted friends, especially a girlfriend. In order to get a girlfriend, he passed out cards printed with his name and address. On each card, he wrote, "If you want to have a good time, call me." He could not understand why women found this offensive. As a result of such problems with social skills, these people often become depressed loners. They keep to themselves to avoid further embarrassment. Under stress, such persons can have relatively short periods of full-blown schizophrenic symptoms, during which they may have hallucinations and frightening delusions. This eruption of symptoms will then go away after the stress passes.

Schizoid Personality Disorder. Much like the schizotypal personality, these people also show odd, eccentric thinking. They are usually mildly paranoid. Unlike the schizotypal personality, they genuinely *do not* want friends or relationships. They want nothing to do with people and avoid social contact. They rarely seek treatment because they are usually content to be left alone. Like those people who have schizotypal personality, periods of schizophrenic symptoms can appear when under stress.

Paranoid Personality Disorder. This disorder is just like it sounds. People with this diagnosis are unrealistically suspicious and distrustful all of the time, far beyond what might be considered a "healthy" mistrust. These people assume that anyone with whom they have contact is trying to trick them, manipulate them, or get something from them. Of course, there is no evidence this is really happening (if there was, they wouldn't be paranoid). They rarely become close with anyone because they trust no one. They are quick to misinterpret innocent actions or comments as proof of their fears. They will hold grudges forever. They tend to be set in their ways and resist any change. They are very self-sufficient and prefer to rely on others as little as possible. Therefore, relationships are avoided or kept very superficial. While people with paranoid personality generally do not hallucinate or have extreme delusions, under stress, they can have brief periods (a few hours or a day) when they lose contact with reality and may have symptoms of schizophrenia. But these go away as the level of stress decreases.

Delusional Disorder. These people have delusions, sometimes severe, without the other symptoms of schizophrenia. For instance, they might believe that they are an informant for the FBI or that the electric company is spying on them through electrical appliances. What makes them different from those suffering from paranoid personality is that they don't have to be *generally* suspicious. The people with paranoid personality are suspicious and distrustful, but don't necessarily put it all together into a delusional system.

Schizophreniform Disorder. This term is used if the person only recently has shown the symptoms of schizophrenia. If the symptoms persist beyond six months, it is then considered schizophrenia.

Schizophrenia, Paranoid Type. While the person has the symptoms of schizophrenia (thought disorder, hallucinations, affective disturbance), the predominant issues involve delusions and hallucinations of being harassed, followed, persecuted, or somehow harmed or threatened. Delusions can be very elaborate and complicated. Further, no amount of reasoning can convince the person their delusion is untrue.

Schizophrenia, Catatonic Type. The patient appears to become "stuck," both physically and mentally. The person may sit in roughly the same position for hours, getting up only when pressured to do so. Often, this reflects a kind of extreme indecision. For instance, one man would remain in the doorway of his room. He later explained that he couldn't decide whether to go in or out. Another woman would sit at the dinner table with her fork hovering over the plate. She later explained that she couldn't decide what to eat. For reasons not entirely clear, this condition is relatively unusual nowadays.

Schizophrenia, Disorganized Type. As the name implies, these people are characterized by their confusion and disorganization. They may speak fluently, but the words make little or no sense. When interviewed, they may repeatedly ask that the question be repeated. There are very long delays in their responses, sometimes as long as minutes. It may take a long time for them to answer a simple question like their name or where they live. This may be due to uncertainty or difficulty in forming an answer. They may be quite uncertain of even simple things, such as their address or whether they have children or have been married. This condition was called "Hebrephrenic Schizophrenia" in older versions of the DSM.

Schizophrenia, Undifferentiated Type. This is a category for people who have some of the symptoms of two or more different types of schizophrenia, but do not clearly fit into any *one* of the above types. For instance, a person may have paranoid delusions, but also show periods of confusion and disorganization.

Schizoaffective Disorder. Many people who have symptoms of schizophrenia also have significant problems with mood instability or extremes of their emotions. Some vary between being very hyper and being depressed. Some become deeply depressed and suicidal. Sometimes the moods are related to their delusions. One man I knew would be elated on days that he heard voices telling him he was "saved by God" and assigned to choose those who would go to heaven with him. On other days, he would be extremely anxious and worried because he was told that he was to choose those to be placed in eternal hell. He would later become suicidal when he heard voices telling him he had angered God and that he himself was condemned to eternal damnation. Some schizoaffective patients I have seen show their "elevated mood" in a negative way, meaning that they can be hostile, angry, and threatening. The key is that there are problems with mood in addition to the other schizophrenic symptoms.

WHAT CAUSES SCHIZOPHRENIA?

I often hear patients or families wonder about what caused their illness. I have heard patients, families, and sometimes even staff blame the illness on things like the following:

- Bad parenting—parents often worry about what they did wrong to cause this illness.
- Too much stress.
- "He burned out his brain on drugs."

Each of these "theories" *are wrong*.

In years past, there were in fact theories proposing that schizophrenia was caused by a pathological family. In particular, a "schizophrenogenic mother" was blamed as the cause. Subsequent research over the years has shown this to be flat-out wrong. In fact, the "cause" may actually work in the opposite direction. A child, teen, or young adult with a major mental illness is often an enormous stress upon a family. The patient's behavior may actually cause a family to adapt *to the child* in such a way that it begins to *look* pathological to outsiders. However, it *has* been found that families which are particularly high in emotional expression can make schizophrenic symptoms worse. However, this is not the same as *causing* schizophrenia.

Stress and trauma can certainly cause mental health problems, including depression, anxiety, posttraumatic stress disorder, and even personality changes. However, people who suffer the most severe stress (such as war, terrible accidents, severe childhood abuse, etc.) rarely develop schizophrenia. However, if a person begins to experience schizophrenic symptoms, a severe stress can easily precipitate or set off the first "psychotic break." In fact, there is often a "last straw." Normal life stresses that are usually part of young adulthood can set off an illness that is already kind of lurking in the background. These are events such as starting college, moving away from home, a relationship breakup, or entering the military. Recall that the onset of symptoms is in the teens or twenties. While at home, in a familiar environment, facing familiar day-to-day problems, a teen may be able to cope with some schizophrenic symptoms (such as some paranoia or hearing voices). Therefore, they seem like they are doing okay. However, the challenges that typically are a part of young adulthood (such as moving away from home, college, rejection by a boyfriend or girlfriend) can suddenly place a greater demand on mental and emotional functioning. Because of the schizophrenia, the person may already be functioning at maximum capacity while dealing with the familiar demands. An increase in demands, especially new and unfamiliar ones, can then become an overload, which triggers the initial breakdown and the first obvious episode of illness. But remember that the stress itself was not the real cause. The stress merely exposed the problem that had been percolating, like pouring gasoline on a smoldering fire.

Similarly, street drugs are usually not the *cause* of schizophrenia. Street drugs such as cocaine and amphetamines can actually cause *symptoms of* paranoia, delusions, and hallucinations and therefore produce a brief "drug-induced psychosis." These symptoms go away as the drug is eliminated from the body, resulting in the remission of symptoms in just a few days. However, these drugs, as well as marijuana, serve to make schizophrenic symptoms worse for a person who has the disorder. This is not the same as *causing* schizophrenia. Hallucinogens, such as LSD, can cause hallucinations and delusions. Sometimes these symptoms return even when the person is not using the drug (flashbacks). However, these experiences usually have a different quality from those of schizophrenia. Furthermore, symptoms go away between episodes of drug use or between flashbacks.

The actual cause of schizophrenia appears to be in the genetic code that we inherit from our parents. This code is carried in a very complex molecule called DNA, which is found in every cell in our body. Each person's DNA contains a virtual blueprint for the construction of every aspect of our body. This includes our height, eye and hair color, and, most important for our purposes here, the way each person's brain is designed, organized, and set up to develop. While everyone's brain is pretty similar, seemingly small differences in structure, organization, and function can make a big difference in how we feel, act, and think. For instance, damage to an area of your brain smaller than a dime could cause a huge loss in your ability to remember things or to use language.

Let me get back to the idea that at least part of the cause of schizophrenia lies in this inherited genetic code. This is shown by the fact that this disorder runs in families. The frequency of schizophrenia in the general population is 1 to 2 percent. (It is interesting that this rate is about the same all over the world, in any country, for any ethnic group.) However, if one parent has schizophrenia, the chances are about 16 percent that their child will also be diagnosed with schizophrenia. If both parents have schizophrenia, the chance of a child having schizophrenia increases to about 33 percent. The chances that the brother or sister of a person diagnosed with schizophrenia will also have schizophrenia is about 14 percent. However, the odds increase to around 50 percent if the brother/sister who has schizophrenia is an identical twin, which is someone who has the identical genetic code. It is important to add that these figures are much the same whether the patient was raised with the biological family or in an adopted family. For example, if one identical twin has schizophrenia, the other twin will have schizophrenia about 50 percent of the time, regardless if the twins live in the same home or not. This is a compelling argument for a genetic cause. However, it is also important to note that even though identical twins have the same genes, the environment plays an important part. One role for the environment may be in triggering the onset. Another role may involve the development of life skills that help the person accept and cope with the illness.

There is very probably more than one gene that contributes to schizophrenia. There are probably many genes. These genes determine the development and functioning of the brain. Therefore, they play a crucial part in the evolution of schizophrenia. This "multiple gene" theory helps explain why a person can have schizophrenia when neither parent has the symptoms, or why schizophrenic parents can have normal children. Let's say there are ten genes involved in producing schizophrenia, and you must have at least four of them to show symptoms. If each parent has three genes, neither will show symptoms (but might seem a little odd, as in schizotypal personality disorder). If you get all three from each parent, you will have six genes and therefore show symptoms of schizophrenia. In the same example, your brother might not inherit any of the genes and so have no signs of schizophrenia. This multiple gene idea may also help explain the enormous differences in the severity of symptoms. For instance, those with only four of the genes have fairly mild symptoms, while those who get all ten genes have the most severe symptoms. There may also be genes that determine the type of symptom a person will experience.

Over the years, there have been many theories about other causes of schizophrenia. These include various infections, environmental poisons, and even vaccinations. None of these have really panned out. However, it is still possible that there are multiple causes of what we call schizophrenia, some of which are not genetic. It may also be that the one condition we have been calling schizophrenia could really be several different but similar disorders, all with different causes. This could explain the differences we see in types of symptoms and in the course the disorder takes.

Whichever the cause or causes of schizophrenia may be, they *operate* in the *brain*. Therefore, in order to understand schizophrenia, a rudimentary understanding of brain function is necessary.

THE BRAIN

The workings of the brain determine what we see, hear, feel, and think. It is actually our *brain* that tells us what is happening and what we are doing. For instance, let's consider a sound. A drum is beating. This causes the air to vibrate, causing a sound wave. This sound wave makes my eardrum vibrate, which causes a very small electrical signal to move up my auditory nerve to the auditory sensory areas of my brain. This part of my brain processes the information and concludes that I am hearing a drum. Usually, this system works fine. Usually there *is* a drum making the sound that my brain interprets as a drum. However, suppose that we could do an operation on my head and expose the particular part of my brain that is responsible for perceiving sound. If we gently stimulate this auditory sensory area in my brain by using a very small electrical current, I would *also* hear a drum. I would hear the drum because that area of my brain was stimulated, even though there is actually no drum! It is important to realize that in each case, the sound I *experience* could be exactly the same to me. In each case, my *brain* tells me there is the sound of a drum. I have no way of knowing whether this is from a real drum (outside of my brain) or from inside my brain (a hallucination). My only clue is whether I can *see* that there is a drum. If I see no drum, I may try to figure out how I could be hearing a drum when I don't see one. (This is where delusions can come in.) The point is that a sensory experience can be exactly the same, whether it comes from "outside" or "inside."

The same idea can be applied to "thoughts." Hundreds of thoughts, ideas, and images are going through our minds constantly. You have probably become painfully aware of this if you ever tried to meditate. Sometimes you can notice the flood of ideas when you lie down to sleep as well. However, we are usually not aware of these thoughts because our brain automatically screens out the stuff that is irrelevant, nonsensical, or inappropriate. Further, our brain clearly labels "thoughts" (what is *inside*) as distinct from what comes from the *outside*. In schizophrenia, this labeling and filtering system doesn't always work. Therefore, it becomes difficult to distinguish between a thought or fantasy (which comes from inside) and reality (which comes from outside). In this way, a passing fantasy of being the president, which is normally screened out from your awareness, becomes a belief that "I am the president."

Brain Circuits: Neurons and Neurotransmitters

The brain is made up of billions of very tiny units or nerve cells called *neurons*. In a way, they are like the millions of circuits that make up a computer. For our purposes here, neurons have two important parts (see Figure 2 below). There are many tiny branches called *dendrites*. These gather and then transmit information to the body of the cell. The cell then digests this input and transmits a signal out of the cell along a single transmission wire called an *axon*. Axons are long arms or fibers that extend from the nerve cell and send an electrical signal to another cell's dendrite. Some of these axons can be three or four feet long. They are different from dendrites in that they don't have the branches that you see on dendrites. Basically, the axons are the "transmission wires" that send electrical signals away from their own cell bodies to the dendrites of a second cell, which receives the signals and transmits them to its own cell body to be processed.

FIGURE 2
THE NEURON

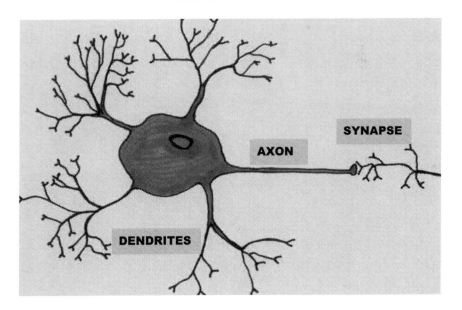

It is important to understand that a neuron can transmit information in only two ways: (1) whether it "fires" or doesn't fire, or (2) the frequency of firing (how fast or slow it fires). The point at which an axon connects with the dendrite of another neuron is called the *synapse*. There are billions of these connections, creating extremely complex circuits. The patterns of activity in these complex circuits are the "cause" of our thoughts, perceptions, and movements.

Another very critical fact is that these "wires" (i.e., the dendrites and axons) *do not actually connect*. Instead, there is a tiny space between them called the *synaptic gap* (see Figure 3 below). So if the two do not connect, how does information get from one neuron to the next? An electrical pulse travels down an axon. When it gets to the end, there is a bulge where special chemicals are stored. These chemicals are called *neurotransmitters*. They are stored in special little bags called *vesicles*. The electrical pulse causes these vesicles to release their chemicals into the synaptic gap. The neurotransmitters float across this gap until they reach a similar bulge at the end of the dendrite nearby. These neurotransmitters then fit into specific holes on the dendrite, like keys into locks. When enough of the keys fit into the right locks, it produces a signal for the dendrite to send its own electrical impulse to its own cell body. When enough of these pulses come into the cell body from its dendrites, a new electrical impulse will be sent down the axon of this neuron to the dendrite of another nerve cell. There are actually many different neurotransmitters, or "keys," that operate in the brain. Some of the ones that you will hear about most often are dopamine, serotonin, and norepinephrine. Particular regions of the brain use one particular neurotransmitter, while other areas of the brain use a different neurotransmitter. This is because each dendrite will only accept a certain "key" into its "lock."

FIGURE 3
THE SYNAPTIC GAP

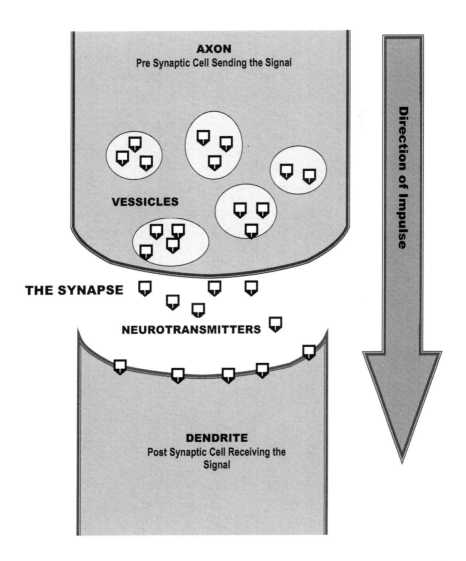

While this is a truly amazing system, there are certainly many things that can go wrong. If there is a shortage of the neurotransmitter, it will be very hard to transmit information across the synapse. Therefore, there may be many axons carrying electrical impulses; but if there is not enough neurotransmitter, there won't be enough "keys" to fill the "locks" on the dendrite in order to make the dendrite start an electrical impulse. On the other hand, if there is far too much of the neurotransmitter floating around in the synapse, then the locks are always getting filled, even if there isn't an electrical impulse coming down the axon to transmit to the dendrite. In other words, if there is too much neurotransmitter in the synapse, the receiving dendrite might "respond" to the axon's message when there actually *was no message*. There can also be dendrites that are hypersensitive to their neurotransmitter or some that are insensitive. It is probably these kinds of "errors" in the brain that cause the symptoms of schizophrenia. These errors could cause a few different kinds of problems. Here are some ideas about how these errors could lead to the symptoms of schizophrenia.

- If the receptors in an area are hypersensitive, the brain might tell me that something is there, when actually there isn't. This could apply to sounds, sights, and even thoughts. This would account for hearing or seeing things that are not really present, which we call hallucinations.
- The brain's natural censor or screening device fails to work. This requires a little explanation. When you lie down to sleep at night, you may become aware of all of

the thoughts going through your head that you hadn't noticed during the day. This is because your brain automatically screens out most of the things that aren't relevant at the moment. For instance, while you are reading this, these words are probably in the foreground of your attention, while everything else fades into the background. You don't notice the physical sensation of the book in your hands or of the chair you are sitting on. You don't notice breathing or swallowing. You are also unaware of the thoughts you may have about your upcoming meal, your plans for the day, or daily problems you have to solve. In fact, there are probably hundreds of thoughts flying through your head that your brain pushes to the background. There are even more thoughts that your brain automatically screens out as irrelevant or very strange. When these thoughts or images do occasionally leak into awareness, you probably say to yourself, "That's really stupid," and dismiss it. For some people with schizophrenia, this screening process doesn't work. *All* of these thoughts and perceptions constantly flood over the person. They are unable to bring the task at hand to the front of their attention. This makes it very hard to concentrate on anything as their attention is constantly being pulled in different directions.

- Let's continue with the "strange thoughts" that are normally screened or dismissed but are not screened out. For instance, while in a store, the thought of stealing something may cross my mind. While I would dismiss this as something I won't do, this can easily become a focus or preoccupation for a person with schizophrenia. They may come to believe that they *have* stolen something and that the police are after them! Similarly, such thoughts can be perceived as being "inserted" by some outside entity.

- The brain can confuse internal and external stimuli, as I discussed earlier. Normally, our brain is able to identify or "label" thoughts as different from what we hear and see. Even if we close our eyes and "imagine" a familiar voice or a favorite song, we know we are not really hearing it. This labeling process can break down. This means that our thoughts (particularly the "strange" ones that should have been screened out) can be labeled as coming from *outside*, rather than being a thought created *inside* our brain. For instance, a thought may float through my head that the FBI could mistake me for a wanted murderer. However, I automatically dismiss this as extremely improbable. This may not be dismissed by the person with schizophrenia. Instead, this thought would be interpreted as reality. As a result, they may become extremely suspicious and fearful that they are being watched by FBI agents, that their house is bugged, and so on.

THE COURSE OF THE ILLNESS

How Does It Start?

Schizophrenia almost always starts before age thirty, although symptoms usually begin in the late teens or early twenties. In some cases, "odd" qualities are noticed in childhood, such as inattention, peculiar ways of thinking, and trouble getting along with people. This is the result of milder symptoms of the illness gradually starting to creep into a person's life. While these symptoms have usually been present for a few years before they are noticed by family and friends, the person may be able to keep the symptoms covered up as long as life is not too demanding. For some people, schizophrenia can begin with trouble concentrating and thinking clearly. Sometimes people with schizophrenia will show odd behavior in grade school, with delusions and hallucinations starting in high school. To the observer, the major symptoms of schizophrenia can seem to start suddenly, often associated with some event. Parents will often tell me that they think that their child's schizophrenia was caused by a stressful event, like being fired from a job, a relationship breakup, or a physical injury. In fact, this event was *not* the *cause*. Rather, the illness had been building for years; and often, one of the normal stresses we all experience in growing up served as a trigger, kind of like the "last straw that broke the camel's back." One example comes to mind. I worked with one man who was captain of his high school football team, kept a B average in high school, and was socially popular. However, within a year of going away to college, he became severely ill. In fact, he had been ill for at least two years, but was able to conceal his symptoms while in the familiar environment of home and school. But the stress of starting college proved to be too much for him, and he had his first schizophrenic episode.

How Does It Progress?

Schizophrenia can take several different courses. I have found that it is usually impossible to predict which course it will take for any given person. The exception is the case in which the symptoms start out early, are severe, and don't respond well to treatment. In these situations, the hallucinations and delusions may diminish over time (or they become less upsetting), but there is a steady decline in general mental functioning. But this is not the typical case. Sometimes the symptoms go away entirely after the first episode, returning only once in a while in times of stress. Another course I have seen is that symptoms start very mild in the teens and gradually worsen until they seem to level off in the thirties. It is also important to understand that the pattern of symptoms often changes. Early on, the person may be just very withdrawn and confused. A few years later, they may become more agitated, obviously delusional, suspicious, and disruptive. At a later point in the course of the disease, they may show big mood changes. So it isn't unusual for the pattern or type of symptoms to change.

Here are several distinct directions the illness can go.

- There are some people who have a flare up of symptoms once in a while. These symptoms seem to resolve on their own, without the use of medication (or very little use of medication). Some studies in Europe report that, for some patients, talk therapy and psychoeducation (which will be discussed in a later section) can be more effective than medication in the long run. However, many people do not improve without medication.
- Some people have only periodic episodes, which completely resolve with medication. Once stable, these patients may be able to go off medication once they learn their "warning signs." They can then avoid relapses by resuming their medication when they observe the first hints of symptoms. These people can lead a largely normal life.
- For some, their symptoms can be completely controlled with medication; however, they must remain on medication for the rest of their life. Nonetheless, with good self-care, these people can also lead a largely normal life.
- For some, medications do not completely eliminate symptoms. However, the symptoms can be reduced

to a manageable level. For example, medication may make the voices (i.e., auditory hallucinations) quieter so the patient can more easily ignore them. In another case, the delusions may still be present, but the patient doesn't feel compelled to act on them. Despite these residual problems, many people can maintain some level of employment, live independently, and have a fulfilling social life. Various skills can also be learned that can be used to cope with the symptoms.

- Medications may have only a small effect on symptoms. A great deal of effort and support is needed to cope. The person cannot hold a job, and social relationships are quite limited.

- For a few, there may be a progressive course of deterioration. At first, the symptoms such as paranoia and hallucinations may steadily worsen. Over time, these may lessen, but there is an accompanying mental deterioration that never improves, something like dementia.

What Causes Relapses?

Regardless of the course, it is important to remember that this illness cannot be cured, but it often can be managed. (As noted above, the disorder can occasionally go into remission.) Sometimes it can be managed very well and sometimes not so well. Nonetheless, when treatment is stopped, the symptoms that were under control will usually return. So quitting the medication can be a problem. When people become stable or symptom free on medication, they often believe they are "cured" and stop taking the medication. This usually leads to a relapse within at least a year, but usually within weeks. Frequent relapses are very disruptive to a person's life and social functioning. For instance, repeated hospitalizations make it hard to keep a job or get through school. Further, when people repeatedly relapse, they do not always recover to the same point they were at before the relapse. There is some evidence that repeated relapses may actually worsen the underlying condition. This is why relapse prevention is important.

Drug abuse is another common cause of relapse. Marijuana, cocaine, and stimulants are especially hazardous in triggering a relapse. That is because these drugs affect the parts of the brain involved in schizophrenia. Even a little marijuana or cocaine can easily trigger relapse in a patient who is reliably taking his/her medication.

While the excessive use of alcohol is harmful to anyone, I have not seen alcohol to be especially harmful to people with schizophrenia in respect to relapses. While alcohol does not seem to make schizophrenia worse, it negatively affects judgment for everyone, including people with schizophrenia. In fact, it doesn't take much alcohol to affect judgment. There are many things we consider doing that we quickly realize are a bad idea. We may want to hurt someone out of revenge, tell off our boss, run away, steal a car, or even plan suicide. When we are sober, we usually conclude, "No, that would be stupid." However, even just a couple of alcoholic drinks can affect our judgment so that when considering some of the previous examples, we might instead say, "Oh heck, why not?" That is why alcohol abuse raises the risk of accidents, violence, and suicide attempts. Many, if not most of the people that I have evaluated after a suicide attempt admitted to drinking alcohol before the attempt. It should also be noted that it usually takes far less alcohol to produce intoxication when you are taking psychotropic medications. In other words, you will get drunk faster when you are on medication.

Relapse can also be triggered by stress and poor self-care. This doesn't mean that people with schizophrenia must run from any hint of stress. It just means they have to be able to plan for stress and manage it better than the rest of us. When under stress, most people let their self-care slide. We get less sleep, eat poorly, use more caffeine, stop exercising, begin isolating, do fewer enjoyable things, and, if a smoker, smoke more. This kind of poor self-care is harmful for everyone. However, for a person with schizophrenia, this can lead to a relapse, even if they kept up with their medication. In particular, I have often seen that going without sleep is a very common factor in triggering a relapse. (See the later section on "Beyond Medication" for more on managing stress.)

TREATMENT

Acceptance

The first and most crucial step a patient must make toward recovery is simply *acceptance*. A person first must accept that they *have* an illness before they can be expected to make a serious effort to *take care* of the illness. This applies to any illness. For instance, you cannot manage high blood pressure when you refuse to believe you have hypertension or that it could lead to serious problems if you do not take care of it. We all know people who don't accept their medical problems and therefore become progressively worse. The faulty reasoning goes like this: "If I go to the doctor, he'll tell me I have hypertension. So I just won't go to the doctor. That way, I won't have a problem." The desire to deny is much stronger when the illness involves something so personal as our mind and emotions. All of us would rather believe the "problem" is with everyone else and not with ourselves. Unfortunately, you cannot successfully manage an illness if you refuse to believe you have it. I have seen many people who could be leading fulfilling lives, with a career and family, if only they would take care of their illness. Instead, they refuse to accept and treat their illness. They are constantly fighting *against treatment* rather than *against the illness*. As a result, they are continually in and out of hospitals, they have alienated their family, and they are unable to keep a job and support themselves. In short, the illness has taken over, and the schizophrenia runs the person's life. The goal of treatment is to put the person back in charge of his or her life, so that they run their life, not the illness.

Management of Hallucinations and Delusions

With any of the perceptual problems—such as hearing things, seeing things, or thinking things that are not real—the first step toward successful coping is again understanding and acceptance. You have to tell yourself that these things are happening *in your brain* because of your illness. They are *not* happening in the outside world that everyone else sees. Since symptoms are coming from your own brain, they cannot actually hurt you or anyone else. Over the years, patients have shared with me the different ways they try to cope with the "voices" that they hear (i.e., auditory hallucinations). I've also worked with patients to develop a couple of tricks they hadn't thought of. However, a person's auditory hallucinations are not always the same and in fact can often change over the course of a day. Sometimes they are funny, sometimes threatening, sometimes helpful and encouraging, and sometimes encourage violence. Further, the intensity often changes: sometimes they are quiet whispers and easy to ignore, while at other times they are shouting and impossible to ignore.

The biggest problem with delusions is that they *seem* real to the person experiencing them. Therefore, it is hard to realize that you are experiencing delusions. Sometimes people have *some* feeling that their conclusions or ideas don't make sense. For instance, I might feel that the CIA is bugging my house and following me. However, when I think about this, I know I am not doing anything that the CIA would be interested in, so I suspect that this *could* be a delusion. However, it is hard to really believe this because the delusion seems so real. Sometimes delusions dovetail with hallucinations. If I was feeling that the government was spying on me through the TV, this may seem to be confirmed by voices that I might hear talking about me.

The techniques suggested here may work for some hallucinations and/or delusions, but not for others. Often, patients use these methods in various combinations. You will just have to try to see which methods work for you. Since hallucinations are most often auditory, the focus of these techniques is dealing with "voices."

Labeling. For some, it is helpful to simply identify the hallucination for what it is. So when they have a bothersome or upsetting hallucination, they may say to themselves something like this: "This is just a hallucination. It's just some thoughts in my head. It's just brain chemicals out of balance. No one else actually hears this." The same labeling technique can be used with delusions. For instance, "I know that it seems like those people are watching me, but now I know that that feeling is just a delusion. They're just thoughts in my head."

Arguing. Some people find it works to argue or "tell off" the hallucinatory voices they hear. They may tell them to "Shut up," "Be quiet," or "Leave me alone." Sometimes this works, but not always. Some people tell me that this seems like it can sometimes make the voices "mad." It can also cause another problem—you may not want to have people see you talking to the air. So if you can't limit your argument to thoughts, you will only use this strategy when you are alone.

The use of rational argument can be applied to delusions as well. For instance, "I know it seems like my house is bugged by the government, but there is no reason the government would be spying on me. I'm no one that important, and I'm not doing anything the government would be concerned about." Or if I feel like two people in the coffee shop are watching me and saying critical things about me, I might tell myself, "I've never seen them before, so they probably aren't talking about me. But even if they are, who cares? I don't know them, and I don't care what they think of me."

Distraction. People often find that when they keep busy, they do not notice the hallucinations as much. If you are able to occupy yourself with something like a TV show, a conversation, or a game of cards, it may be easier to ignore the hallucination. Again, if you can ignore the voices for a while, they may just go away. This is why hallucinations can be more of a problem at bedtime. When you are lying in bed, in a dark and quiet room, there is nothing to interfere with the voices that you may have hardly noticed all day.

The "TV commercial" technique. Think of when you are watching a good program on TV, and then a commercial comes on. Do you remember what the commercial is about? Usually not. Typically, you will continue to look at the TV during the commercial, but just let it "go by" without really paying attention to it. Sometimes this can be done with an auditory hallucination—just let it "go by" like a commercial, without really paying attention.

Blocking it out. Many people find that they can just drown out the voices with music. Headphones seem to work best. When you turn up the music, you can't hear the voices anymore. Just be sure to pick music that you like and that it isn't music that upsets you.

Reality testing. This method applies primarily to delusions and paranoia, but can also apply to hallucinations. The idea is to "check out" the perception, fear, or worry with someone you trust to see if it is actually happening. Let's say you're at a store with a good friend who knows about your illness. You get a strange sense that two people are looking at you and laughing like they think you are doing something stupid. In order to see whether this is really happening or just a delusion, you should then "check it out" with your friend. You could ask him or her if it looks like the two people are laughing at you or talking about you. They can help you figure out if something is really going on or if it is just paranoia. Or let's say you heard a voice say something that is insulting to you. You could ask your friend, "Did you hear that?" If he or she says they heard nothing, then it must have been a hallucination.

Another way to test the reality of these delusions is to pay attention to the feedback that you will probably be getting from the people around you, such as family or friends. If everyone around you is telling you that something you are thinking is untrue, it probably is untrue. It's unlikely that *everyone* is lying. If you have some doubt that an idea may be a delusion, check it out with someone you trust.

Visual hallucinations. Visual hallucinations don't seem to occur nearly as often as auditory hallucinations, but they can still be very upsetting. First, if possible, it's smart to perform a "reality test," or check it out with someone you trust. Find out if they see what you are seeing. If it really is a hallucination, there are a couple of things you can try. Sometimes a simple distraction will work, like I described above. If you are busy, you just won't pay much attention to "unreal" things that you are seeing. If the hallucination is upsetting and you can't ignore it, you can sometimes make it go away by involving other senses. Remember that this "vision" is actually a kind of false message your brain is giving you that is caused by the illness. If you try to touch it, the fact that you won't feel anything can make the vision stop. Or you can have someone else go to where you see the vision and try to touch it. The presence of a real person can sometimes "override" the hallucination.

Addressing Hallucinations and Delusions as a Family Member, a Friend, or a Provider

Just as the first step for the patient is their acceptance that they have an illness, the first step in helping a person with schizophrenia is *your acceptance and understanding that their experiences seem absolutely real and reasonable to them.* The voices of a hallucination can seem just as real to the person hallucinating as your voice talking to them. The perception that they are in danger is their reality. Therefore, you must clearly convey that you *believe* that they are truly experiencing these things and that they are not lying or making things up. *Do not say,* "It's all in your head" or "It's just your imagination." Even though this is somewhat correct, it belittles and minimizes what the patient is experiencing. *It is real to them.* Remember, our reality is *really* what our brain tells us is there. The patient's brain may be telling them that there is an unseen voice threatening to kill them. Which are they going to believe—what they actually *hear* or your claim that there is nothing there? Think of what you would do under the circumstances. So here are a few steps to take in helping the person who is experiencing serious schizophrenic symptoms. For example's sake, let's assume that they are having threatening auditory hallucinations that are fairly new (otherwise, the patient may have become fairly accustomed to the voices and may not be as upset).

- First, tell the patient that you can understand that it must be terrifying to hear what they tell you they are hearing, adding that you do not hear it. If they ask how you know what they are hearing if you can't hear it, remind them that *they told you. "There is no way for me to know what is inside your mind unless you tell me."*

- Help them figure out why this could be happening. The first reason that they usually propose is that you are lying. However, if they find that no one else hears the voice either, it would seem unlikely that *everyone* is lying. Therefore, it may be that the things they are hearing exist *only* inside their mind.
- Emphasize that you want to help them make the voices stop bothering them and disappear. You can add that you can imagine how terrible this is. Or you can say that you have been told by other people that have this problem that hearing voices is very hard to put up with.
- They may be relieved to know other people have the same problem and that they are not alone, so they can conclude, "Maybe I'm not crazy."

Medication Use

Unfortunately, while in the grip of psychosis, a person is often unable to realize that they have an illness causing their problems. Therefore, medication use is often necessary before the patient is able to even try to address the issue of acceptance. While there are psychological techniques and skills that can be used to manage and control schizophrenic symptoms, these don't really do much about the neurochemical problems in the brain that are causing the symptoms. Because of the biological roots of schizophrenia, medication use is often at the core of treatment and recovery. Without the reduction of the perceptual, mental, and emotional symptoms, it is impossible to use other coping skills or address other issues of self-concept, self-care, education, or employment. Because of the importance of medication, I will devote the next section to medication use.

MEDICATION

The Theory behind Medication

The information about neurotransmitters I explained earlier suggests that the "errors" made by the brain could be corrected. For instance, if neurons in one area of the brain are hypersensitive to the neurotransmitter dopamine, there should be a way to "calm down" this hypersensitivity. Similarly, there should be ways to make adjustments when there is too much or too little of a particular neurotransmitter. This is in fact the theory behind medication use for schizophrenia as well as other mental illnesses, such as depression and bipolar disorder. The medications used to treat schizophrenia are called "antipsychotic" medications. Sometimes the term "neuroleptic" is used as well. Unfortunately, the identification of the exact neurotransmitter receptors involved in schizophrenia has proven to be an extremely complex problem. Further complicating the issue, each neurotransmitter has several different *kinds* of receptors. In addition, there are likely to be *several* combinations of neurotransmitter receptors involved, which may not be the same for each person. As a result, there are many different antipsychotic medications. Each addresses a somewhat different combination of neurotransmitter receptors. Unfortunately, each drug also affects additional neurotransmitter receptors that are not involved with schizophrenia. It's a little like shooting at a squirrel with a shotgun. While you probably hit the squirrel, you also hit lots of other things too. The degree to which this happens determines the side effects that the drug will produce, such as sleepiness, restlessness, or nausea. There is a delicate balancing act between affecting the receptors you *want* to target versus steering clear of the receptors that will cause side effects. Think of your lawn as another example. You want to stop the crabgrass and dandelions from growing and taking over your lawn. However, the chemicals that destroy the weeds can also kill the grass or flowers that you've planted. The trick is to find a chemical that destroys only the weeds, but doesn't kill the grass and flowers.

Some medications like Haldol are good at affecting most of the relevant receptors. Unfortunately, like using the above shotgun, Haldol hits the desired targets, but also hits everything else nearby. As a result, Haldol is quite effective in reducing symptoms like hallucinations and delusions. However, it is also one of the medications that will most likely cause uncomfortable side effects. Other medications that produce very few side effects are not particularly effective for many people in reducing symptoms.

Types of Medication

Medications are variously referred to by either their chemical name or their brand name. A common household example is the brand name Tylenol, whose chemical or generic name is acetaminophen. This can be very confusing. For simplicity's sake, I will generally refer to drugs by their brand name.

Antipsychotic medications have improved enormously over the last twenty years. When I started practicing in the early 1980s, there were quite a number of antipsychotic medications. Unfortunately, they all caused the same kinds of uncomfortable side effects, sooner or later. Some of these side effects could be permanent. Therefore, it was very difficult for a patient to choose between potentially unpleasant side effects and the symptoms of schizophrenia. As you may guess, it was also very difficult to convince people to stay on their medication. Now there are more choices, most of which involve fewer and milder side effects. Some antipsychotic medications are made in alternative forms, which can be useful for some patients. Some come in liquid form. A quickly dissolving, "melt in your mouth" tablet is made for two of the newer medications (Zyprexa and Risperdal). Long-lasting injectable forms are available for Haldol, Prolixin, and Risperdal. This is useful for patients who either forget their pills or are resistive to taking oral medications. Several medications are also made in a short-acting injectable form.

Antipsychotic medications are roughly classified into two groups: The older medications are patterned after the first antipsychotic, Thorazine, and are called "typical" antipsychotic medications. The relatively newer medications developed since the introduction of Clozaril are called "atypical" antipsychotic medications.

"Typical" antipsychotic medications. The era of antipsychotic medication started in 1953 with the introduction of Thorazine (chlorpromazine is the generic name). This revolutionized treatment. For the first time, there was a tool that actually reduced symptoms for many people. Until then, all that could be done was to segregate mentally ill patients from the rest of the population. Various treatments had been tried. Psychotherapy was used, but only worked with people whose symptoms were mild or who were not really suffering from schizophrenia. Barbaric-sounding things, such as psychosurgery (sometimes called "lobotomies") were done as well. Insulin shock treatments were used, which generally didn't help and could too often be fatal. So you can see that despite the side effects, Thorazine was a big improvement. The effectiveness of Thorazine allowed many people to be discharged from long-term hospitalization. This also resulted in a big improvement in the quality of life for many patients. However, this movement to "deinstitutionalize" also led to "dumping" people on to the street who had spent much of their life in institutions. Therefore, many of these newly discharged patients lacked the skills to live independently and ended up homeless or in jail. But this is a topic for another book. Because of the success of Thorazine, numerous drugs were developed over the next twenty years or so in an attempt to refine the antipsychotic effects of Thorazine. Many of these are no longer available. Here are a few of the ones that were commonly used.

Mellaril
Navane
Stelazine
Loxitane (Loxipine)
Serentil
Prolixin
Haldol

The last two on this list, Prolixin and Haldol, are still used with some frequency and require some further discussion. Both are still commonly used and are quite effective in reducing some of the symptoms of schizophrenia. They both have significant side effects as well (see below). They are valuable, however, because both can be given in a long-acting injectable form called "decanoate." Sometimes people have trouble remembering to take oral medication and then relapse. Sometimes patients who are very paranoid or refuse to accept their illness may lie about taking pills on their own. Even when monitored, some manage to spit out or avoid taking pills. Therefore, a shot that lasts for one to four weeks can be extremely useful in preventing relapses and so enable them to live outside of a hospital.

"Atypical" antipsychotic medications. Since the 1990s, a whole new class of medications has been developed, starting with Clozaril. Two of these have forms that melt as soon as you put them in your mouth. These are Risperdal M-Tabs and Zydis, which is a "meltable" form of Zyprexa. Risperdal also comes in a long-acting injectable form that lasts for two weeks called Consta. However, once you get an injection of Consta, you still have to take the pills for about two to three weeks until the injection "gets into your system." Geodon and Zyprexa also have injectable forms, but they are only short acting. That is, the effect does not last any longer than taking the pills.

While these "new generation" medications generally are not as potent as Haldol, they have far fewer side effects. Furthermore, no single medication will work for everyone. It is not uncommon that a patient will need to try more than one of these atypical antipsychotics to find one that works well. Sometimes it is necessary to use more than one in combination. Most of these medications have *sedation* as a possible side effect; that is, they will make you sleepy. This often passes as you get accustomed to the medication. Or the sedation can be managed by taking most of the medication before bed so that sleepiness is helpful rather than a problem. An important benefit offered by these atypical antipsychotic medications is that they rarely cause some of the "movement disorders," such as tardive dyskinesia, as a side effect. Akathesia (a kind of restlessness and nervousness) and dystonia (muscle stiffness) are also rare in my experience for all but Risperdal. (See upcoming section on "Potential Side Effects" for an explanation of these side effects.) These side effects are common with the older typical antipsychotic medications. *All* of these medications (both typical and atypical) can have significant weight gain as a side effect. While some studies show Seroquel to be the least likely to cause weight gain, it still happens most of the time. One other problem with these "new generation" medications is that they are much more expensive than the older medications. For instance, Zyprexa may cost $3 a pill, while Haldol may cost less than 10¢ per pill. The trick in prescribing is to find the medication that works the best for any given person, with the least side effects. The biggest problem is that a given medication does not produce the same treatment effect and same side effects for everyone. Zyprexa may be a wonder drug for one person, removing all of their symptoms with no side effects. For another person, it may work well, but cause extreme sedation, even at low doses. For yet another person, Zyprexa may not help at all. Similarly, the dosage required may vary. One person may do well on five milligrams of Zyprexa, while another may require twenty-five milligrams to get a therapeutic effect. And to make things more confusing, the effective medications and dosages for a given person can change over time. For these and other reasons, an effective prescriber must be knowledgeable of the research literature, but must also be very attuned to the patient's response to the medication. (See table 1 for a list of these medications and their brand and generic names.)

Table 1
Trade Names and Chemical/Generic Names of Common Typical and Atypical Antipsychotic Medications

First-Generation / Typical Antipsychotic Medication	Second-Generation / Atypical Antipsychotic Medication
Thorazine (chlorpromazine)	Abilify (aripiprazole)
Haldol (haloperidol) *Haldol Decanoate*	Clozaril (clozapine)
Prolixin (fluphenazine) *Prolixin Decanoate*	Geodon (ziprasidone)
Italics indicate the long-acting injectable form. * indicates a "melt in your mouth" form	Risperdal (risperidone) Risperdal M-Tabs* *Risperdal Consta*
	Invega (paliperidone, a metabolite of risperidone)
	Seroquel (quetiapine)
	Zyprexa (olanzapine) Zydis*

Clozaril requires a few extra comments. When this was first used in Europe, it was seen as a miracle drug because it helped about one-third of the patients who did not benefit from any of the other known medications. Later, Clozaril was found to cause a blood-related side effect called "agranulocytosis" in about 1 percent of those taking it. If undetected, this condition can be fatal. However, these serious effects can be entirely prevented with weekly blood tests. Obviously, weekly blood tests are quite inconvenient. Therefore, it is necessary to weigh the inconvenience against the possible benefits. Clozaril has other unpleasant side effects, including sedation, weight gain, and excessive salivation. However, it remains the only effective medication for some patients. I have seen Clozaril help patients who were incapacitated by their paranoia and hallucinations. A few became entirely free of symptoms. I talked to one particular patient about the annoying side effects he had—in his case, sedation and hypersalivation. *He* told me that he thought that it was a relatively small price to pay to have his life back!

Potential Side Effects of Antipsychotic Medications

Sedation, or sleepiness, is by far the most common side effect. It can happen with both the typical and atypical medications. This can also be managed by adjusting the dose to a lower amount, dividing the dose into two smaller ones eight or ten hours apart, or taking the medication shortly before bedtime. If taken before bedtime, the sedation won't affect daytime activities and may promote sleep if there is a problem with insomnia. Abilify is marketed as an antipsychotic that rarely causes sedation. In fact, it may even have an energizing effect and cause insomnia if taken at night. However, it does make *some* people sleepy.

Akathesia refers to a sense of restlessness. This is common with the older medications, but can sometimes (although rarely) occur with the "new generation" medications as well. People experiencing akathesia tell me they "can't sit still." They may pace constantly or jiggle their legs. Some people say they feel like their "skin is crawling." Some people experience it as anxiety. Sometimes this can be especially noticeable at night when trying to fall asleep, resulting in insomnia. For some, the restlessness can be more of an internal subjective feeling rather than something as obvious as pacing. Often, medications like Benadryl are given to relieve akathesia. When this doesn't work or the side effects of the Benadryl are a problem (sleepiness), it may be necessary to change to a different side effect medication or eventually a different antipsychotic medication. Some of the other common medications used to reduce akathesia are Cogentin, Artane, Symetrel, and Ativan. These medications can also have their own side effects.

Dystonia refers to a stiffening or tightening of the muscles. Again, this side effect is rare with the atypical, 2nd generation medications, but fairly common with the older "typical" antipsychotic medications. Sometimes this side effect is relatively subtle. People may notice a stiffness or soreness in their back, neck, legs, or arms. They may not automatically associate this stiffness or pain with the medication, believing that their bed is too soft or that they may have strained a muscle. However, if it really is dystonia, the problem can be traced to the start of medication use. This muscle discomfort can be resolved quickly with a medication such as Cogentin. Sometimes the stiffness is quite severe. One extreme reaction is called an "ocular crisis," in which the eyes roll upward involuntarily. While potentially frightening, such reactions can be relieved quickly with an injection of Cogentin. When using the older typical antipsychotic medication like Haldol, some prescribers will automatically order Cogentin along with the antipsychotic medication in order to prevent such side effects in the first place.

Weight gain is also common with all of the antipsychotics, both typical and atypical. The worst culprits are Zyprexa and Clozaril. While all of the antipsychotics are associated with weight gain, Geodon, Abilify, and Seroquel seem to be a little less bad. On average, people gain ten to eleven pounds within the first ten weeks of medication. While the weight gain appears to be related to an increase in appetite and a decrease in activity, these medications may also have an effect on a person's metabolism. In other words, antipsychotic medications may also affect weight by influencing how the body processes and uses the food we eat. It is important to note that *everyone* does not gain a lot of weight and that this side effect can be controlled somewhat with diet and exercise. Some studies have suggested a possible link between these medications, weight gain, and the development of diabetes. Associated with gaining weight is the elevation of cholesterol and triglycerides, which can lead to high blood pressure and heart problems. This pattern of symptoms is called *metabolic syndrome* when they all appear together. Often, your doctor will want to do regular checks on your cholesterol, triglycerides, and blood sugar in order to minimize your risks of cardiovascular problems. *This is a topic you should discuss with your doctor in depth.*

Tardive dyskinesia is a more serious side effect that sometimes comes with the long-term use of the older typical medications. This is sometimes an irreversible neurological condition that is often noticed when the medication is reduced or stopped. It is characterized by involuntary facial (especially tongue and mouth) and hand movements. This condition is quite rare when using the newer atypical antipsychotic medications like Zyprexa and Abilify.

Neuroleptic malignant syndrome (NMS) is rare, but can be very serious. Symptoms include elevated temperature, rapid increases and decreases in blood pressure, perspiration, tachycardia (heart racing), tremor, confusion, and sometimes incontinence. While any of the antipsychotic medications can potentially cause NMS, the association is more often with the high-potency typical antipsychotics such as Haldol. High doses or rapid dose increases are also risk factors. This reaction usually appears within the first week or so of treatment. Immediate medical attention is important when signs of NMS appear. However, the condition usually clears quickly when the medication is stopped and medical care is initiated. It is important to remember that this is a fairly rare reaction and that it is easily treated once diagnosed. Further, an occurrence of NMS does not at all rule out the use of antipsychotic medications. However, doses must be started low and increased gradually. It is important that you tell the person prescribing your medication if you have ever had NMS.

Other Types of Medications Used

A few other medications are often used along with antipsychotic medications, either to enhance the antipsychotic effect or to relieve other symptoms associated with schizophrenia. A *mood stabilizer* such as Depakote, Lithium, or Tegretol may be used if the patient is also experiencing intense or rapidly changing moods. (It is interesting that two of these, Tegretol and Depakote, are also used to treat seizure disorders.) *Antianxiety or anxiolytic* medications such as Ativan or Klonopin may be used on a short-term basis to reduce the extreme agitation and anxiety that accompany acute symptoms like paranoia. As described above, these are sometimes used to treat the side effects of the antipsychotic medications.

Other Possible Medication Problems

I have listed and described some of the most common side effects. However, there is a related issue that is important to keep in mind. Medications *interact* with each other. The use of one medication can affect the action and effectiveness of another. Even simple medications like Tylenol or antacids (like Tums) can affect the levels of these antipsychotics and mood stabilizers in your system. If a level is too low in your blood stream, the medication won't work; however, if the level is too high, it could be harmful. Therefore, specialized knowledge about medication interactions is very important. This is usually something that both pharmacists and psychiatrists know a lot about. But they can't read your mind, so make sure that they know about any other pills that you are taking.

Your Working Relationship with a Psychiatrist

The effectiveness of these medications can become meaningless unless you have a solid working relationship with a good psychiatrist or other prescriber. While any physician can legally prescribe these medications (such as your family doctor), I feel it is best to work with someone who is very familiar with these medications. This includes knowledge of their effectiveness, side effects, and interaction with other drugs. Psychiatrists have far more experience in this area than do other physicians. Further, some psychiatrists have far more experience working specifically with antipsychotic medications than do other psychiatrists who might only rarely work with people suffering from schizophrenia. Therefore, be sure to find a prescriber who has a lot of experience working with patients who have schizophrenia.

In addition to the importance of knowledge and experience, also keep in mind that this doctor is someone with whom you will be working closely. There is a good deal of research that indicates that the relationship you have with your doctor (be it a family doctor or psychiatrist or nurse practitioner) has as much to do with the effectiveness of treatment as does the actual medications they prescribe. So it is essential that you find a psychiatrist with whom you feel comfortable as a working partner *against* the schizophrenia. Assuming that you are doing your part to manage your illness, you need a doctor who listens to your observations and uses the information that you provide to make medication adjustments. For instance, if you say the pills make you so sleepy during the day that you can't get anything done (or manage your job or school), they should pay attention to your concern and try to do something about it. They might reschedule the dose so that you take most of it at bedtime. This way, sleepiness won't be a problem. If the psychiatrist does not seem to care that you are too sleepy to manage your job or that you feel sick to your stomach after each dose, then you should look for another doctor. That said, you have to be reasonable in your approach to medication. No one will take you seriously if you complain about *every* appropriate medication or insist *every* medication causes intolerable side effects or insist on using inappropriate drugs like marijuana or Ativan (which is a controlled substance and can be addictive).

Psychiatrists May Not Be Your Only Choice of Prescriber

Family doctors and internists. These are medical doctors who have not specialized in the treatment of mental illness, but rather in the care of medical conditions. Nonetheless, they can legally prescribe antipsychotic medications, as well as any other medications for mental health purposes. If you have a good relationship with your family doctor, there are some advantages of working with him or her. But generally, nonpsychiatrists have very little experience with antipsychotic medications and treating side effects.

Nurse practitioners. These are nurses who have advanced, specialized training. Some have specialized training in the use of medications so that they are qualified to legally prescribe medications for mental health problems such as schizophrenia. While there are not terribly many of these specially trained nurses around, they can be a great alternative. Their training in nursing provides them with a general medical background, while their patient-care orientation often means that nurse practitioners will spend a little more time with their patients and may be more sensitive to patient concerns. In the event of a very complicated case involving both mental health and medical issues, a nurse practitioner will usually consult with a physician.

Psychologists. In a few parts of the United States (such as New Mexico, Louisiana, and Guam), specially trained psychologists are legally qualified to prescribe medications for mental health conditions. Such persons have completed a doctorate in clinical or counseling psychology, are licensed, and have three years of actual experience working in mental health beyond their degree. This means that they have a great deal of knowledge about mental health diagnosis and treatment. It also means that that they are very familiar with methods of treatment besides medication. They then receive two to three years of education and training in psychopharmacology and the medical issues and practices that go along with the prescription of medication. Legislation is being introduced in several other states—including Illinois, Montana, and Wisconsin—to allow these specially trained psychologists to prescribe.

The Decision to Use Antipsychotic Medication

As you can see, the use of medication is a complicated issue. While there are usually clear benefits in terms of symptom relief, there are also significant risks and costs in terms of both short-term and long-term side effects. The real key is finding ways to balance these risks and benefits. You certainly want to make use of all of the self-care practices I will be discussing in sections to come. These techniques and practices will probably *reduce* the amount of medication that will be needed. Even so, the use of medication is a critically important discussion you must have with your prescriber on an ongoing basis. Here are some key questions to address.

At what point do you need medication to get the symptoms under control? How bad do you let things get before you use medications to control the hallucinations and delusions? Keep in mind that if you let things go too far, you will no longer be well enough to make the decision to get treatment. You may reach the point that you think the hallucinations are real, and therefore, you will be unable to make a rational decision. At this point, the decision may be made *for you* by others, such as the Court. Most people prefer to stay well enough so that they can avoid this and retain the ability to make decisions for themselves.

Can I go off medications when I'm doing well? Sometimes people can do this. It works when people are very aware of their warning signs so that they can resume medication as soon as symptoms begin to worsen. That way they can prevent a full-blown relapse. If you quickly get worse after stopping the medication or cannot predict when you are going to relapse, you may need to stay on the medication indefinitely.

The medication that has the least side effects doesn't work as well as the one that has more side effects. The balance between side effects and effectiveness is a very important ongoing discussion to have with your provider. Consider that some side effects may be more tolerable for you than others or that there are some that are less acceptable at certain times (such as sedation during final exam week).

If you are expecting a stressful period, you may want to consider a medication adjustment *before* the stress hits. Sometimes you can see stress coming. It may be a painful anniversary, a seasonal increase in demands at work, or an upcoming court date. If you and your prescriber make adjustments beforehand, you can often get through the stressful period without a relapse.

BEYOND MEDICATION: SELF-CARE AND COPING WITH SYMPTOMS

In some ways, schizophrenia spectrum disorders can be easier to deal with than other mental health problems like posttraumatic stress disorder. Since schizophrenia is fundamentally a physical disorder, recovery seems to be as simple as taking a few pills. But it isn't really that easy.

Before a person can manage an illness, they first have to admit and accept that they have it. This isn't as easy as it sounds. Many people find it very hard to accept that they have simple medical conditions like asthma or hypertension. Kids with asthma often will refuse to take their medication to prevent asthma attacks because they will not *accept* that there is "anything wrong" with them. As a result, they keep having asthma attacks. So if it is hard to accept something like asthma, it must be a lot harder to accept that you have schizophrenia. Many patients will insist, "I'm not crazy!" Mental illness carries a stigma or stereotype that makes it a lot harder to accept. But you *have* to accept it; otherwise, the illness will take over your life. The treatment goal is for *the patient*—*not* the illness—to be in charge of your life. If you can take charge, the illness can be managed and pushed into the background so that you can get on with the business of living your life. Here are a few tips to accepting, coping, and managing the illness.

Knowledge Is Power

The more you know about your illness, the more you can control it. If you choose to be ignorant about your illness, the illness will run your life. Further, you will be unable to judge if your doctor or mental health professionals are giving you good advice. Become an expert on your illness. Read, go to support groups, and ask questions when you see your doctor, nurse, or therapist. Know what to expect from your medications, both positive and negative effects.

Privacy

People in general do not understand schizophrenia spectrum disorders. People fear what they do not understand. For instance, many uninformed people assume incorrectly that people with schizophrenia are dangerous or mentally slow. This is simply untrue. People with schizophrenia are, on average, less dangerous to others than the general population. (However, it should be noted that the rate of suicide is greater for people with schizophrenia than for the general population.)

Therefore, it is important to realize that you don't have to share your diagnosis with everyone. In fact, I'd suggest you share it only with a very few people that you can trust. Besides, with the schizophrenia under control, it is not the most important thing about you. You don't have to introduce yourself, "Hi, I'm Greg. I'm schizophrenic." You are not lying if you simply do not mention your illness.

Manage Your Stress

People with schizophrenia can become overloaded more quickly than other people. Remember, one of the basic problems is processing information. If there is just too much to process, it is possible to trigger a relapse. "Too much" can mean work or school demands, moving, or a sudden increase in family responsibilities. Strong emotions can add to the "overload" as well. For instance, the death of a loved one or the breakup of a relationship can lead to strong and prolonged emotional states. Even if the loss does not require a big increase in responsibility, the emotional intensity alone can be overwhelming if a person has schizophrenia.

Does this mean that people with schizophrenia cannot have any stress in their lives? Absolutely not. However, if you have schizophrenia, you have to be *smarter* about *managing* the stress. For instance, you will have to look ahead to see busy times coming, plan for them, and spread out the demands over time. That way, you don't take on everything at once. If you're in school, don't wait until the deadline to do your work. Instead, plan ahead so you don't have to panic before midterms or the end of the semester. Don't pull all-nighters, cramming for finals or finishing papers. Instead, plan and get the work done ahead of time. This is really important in controlling schizophrenia because sleep deprivation (going without sleep) is often a trigger for relapse. The same applies to work or home projects. Plan to do a little at a time and spread the job out. Don't try to do a big project all in one day. If you suffer a loss, you have to be even more active in avoiding isolation, keeping busy, and surrounding yourself with supportive people.

No Street Drugs

Marijuana, cocaine (crack), and stimulants (such as Ritalin, amphetamines, crystal meth) are extremely harmful to persons with schizophrenia spectrum disorders. They all affect brain systems that are involved in the symptoms of schizophrenia. Unfortunately, many people who feel nervous or scared from their paranoia or hallucinations often use *marijuana* to calm themselves. However, they do not notice that the marijuana also makes the voices and paranoia worse! This then makes them more nervous, so they use more marijuana, which makes the symptoms worse and so on. This is why marijuana use almost always leads to a quick relapse. *Cocaine* (or crack) and stimulants can cause paranoia and hallucinations in people who do not even have schizophrenia. For people who do not have schizophrenia, these symptoms resolve as soon as the drug is washed out of their system. But imagine what these drugs do to people who already have those symptoms. Therefore, the use of any of these drugs is like throwing gasoline on a fire for people who have schizophrenia. A condition that is under control will suddenly become severe. And once triggered, it will not subside once the offending drug is washed out.

Many young people with schizophrenia who feel they don't "fit in" may feel more socially comfortable with a group that is into drugs. The person with schizophrenia might not stand out as being so different when hanging out with others whose thinking is mixed up due to their drug use. Further, it may be fun to feel accepted by a group, even if it isn't a very functional one. The problem is that the drug use will make the schizophrenia worse, which will make it even more likely that the symptoms will get so serious that something bad will happen.

In contrast to these drugs, I have observed that *moderate* alcohol use rarely causes a relapse of schizophrenic symptoms, nor does it seem to make the symptoms worse. This is not a license to go and get drunk, however. Alcohol loosens inhibitions. This means that when you use alcohol, you don't think about the effects or consequences of what you do. That's why people do things while intoxicated that they wouldn't do when they are sober and alcohol free. If people are angry or depressed, alcohol often makes that emotion worse. That is why many suicide attempts and fights happen when people are consuming alcohol. For instance, I might consider punching my boss or my wife, but quickly rule that out as a bad idea that I would later regret. But after only one or two drinks, I might instead think, "Oh, what the heck! Why not?" Also, be aware that you may become intoxicated or drunk more quickly because of your medication.

Caffeine

While caffeine is perfectly legal, it is a stimulant and does affect the brain. This means that it makes you more alert and tends to speed you up. Caffeine is in coffee and many teas, as well as many types of soft drinks (most colas have caffeine). One common beverage I know that has a lot of caffeine is Mountain Dew. It seems that many of the patients I see habitually drink a lot of caffeine every day (a big bottle of Pepsi or a couple of twenty-ounce bottles of Dew). It's no wonder that they can't sleep at night or that they feel hyper and jittery during the day. You should avoid caffeine after about six at night to avoid sleep problems. Limit yourself to two twelve-ounce cans of caffeinated soda during the day. It would be best, however, to avoid caffeine altogether. It is just another psychoactive chemical that can affect your brain and interact with your medication. Decaffeinated coffee now tastes just as good as regular coffee. There are many tasty herbal teas that do not have caffeine. The same can't be said for colas, from my experience. You are better off drinking root beer, Sprite, 7 Up, or juice.

Warning Signs

There are usually signs that signal a relapse in symptoms. It is very important to learn these and watch for them so that you can catch the relapse before the symptoms get severe and the illness takes over. The warning signs are not the same for everyone, so you have to learn which apply to you. Here are some examples:

- **Insomnia, or a lot of trouble sleeping.** If you are getting much less than seven or eight hours of sleep a night, this could signal a problem. In fact, many people with schizophrenia often need more than eight hours of sleep a night. Similarly, a big decrease in the amount of sleep you feel you need could signal a relapse. Such a change in sleep pattern is probably the most common early warning sign and is also one of the easiest to notice.
- **Feeling suspicious, more so than others around you.**
- **Return or worsening of auditory hallucinations.** Sometimes auditory hallucinations are fairly quiet when they start to return, sounding like whispers or noises.
- **A return or increase in the frequency or severity of unpleasant and unwanted thoughts in your head.**
- **Friends or family say that you are acting differently.** They may say that you are more irritable, suspicious, or that you are talking oddly and not making sense.
- **You notice more trouble concentrating.**

I want to stress the value of feedback from others. It's often hard to notice that your symptoms are getting worse. A person might feel a little stressed or nervous but may blame it on other people rather than admit their symptoms are returning. But even if you do not notice the change, the people around you, such as your family, certainly will. This feedback may be the only way for you to know that you need help before it's too late and you have to be hospitalized involuntarily.

When you see these warning signs, *get help.* This could involve contacting your psychiatrist and getting an earlier appointment. You may need a medication adjustment. Or you could call your case manager or therapist for help. You also could check into the hospital voluntarily. When people go to the hospital on their own, it usually goes much more smoothly than when they have to be brought in against their will. When the police get involved, it means the relapse has already gone pretty far and that you are no longer in control of your illness. When you sign in yourself, it means you are still in charge of yourself and still in control of the illness.

Social Support

Living with schizophrenia can be very lonely sometimes. It can also get very boring if you are not able to work or go to school. Some people find that they tend to worry, stop their medication, or get into trouble when they have too much empty time on their hands. Most large communities have some organizations that can help with this problem. In Milwaukee, there are two "clubs" that are designed to help persons living in the community with mental illness:

Grand Avenue Club
210 East Michigan Avenue
Milwaukee, WI
414-276-6474

Our Space
525 West Lincoln
Milwaukee, WI
414-383-8921

Each of these organizations offer many different things to do and are staffed (at least in part) by club members who have schizophrenia. For instance, at the Grand Avenue Club, you can do as little or as much as you want. You can simply drop in to socialize. You can take classes to learn some computer skills. You can work on the newsletter or in their business office. They operate a kitchen that serves lunch and does catering. And they have a transitional employment program. This is all free of charge. All you have to do is apply and complete an orientation. Our Space has many similar activities.

These organizations can help you get out of the house and become involved in life again. Some people tell me that they would rather get a job instead. However, it would be wise to start out with one of these clubs. It isn't easy to get a job in the first place. If you are fortunate enough to get a job, employment requires that you meet strict demands. You have to be at work *every* day and be able to function consistently, day in and day out. If you don't show up at your job because you are having a bad day, you will lose the job. An employer doesn't have to be understanding about your mental illness, and they probably won't have much patience if you have symptoms on the job. The clubs, on the other hand, are *designed* for people recovering from mental illness. Therefore, they *do* understand when you have bad days or if your symptoms begin to come back.

WHAT DOES THIS MEAN
FOR MY KIDS?

Schizophrenia is most likely a genetic disorder. The genes (or DNA) you inherit from your parents carry the biological blueprint for the development of your entire body. This includes the development of your brain, both its structure and operation. Recall that the symptoms of schizophrenia are a result of imbalances in the operation of the brain. (See the earlier section on the causes of schizophrenia.) Therefore, the illness often runs in families. This means that you can pass these genes on to your children. However, if you have schizophrenia, the odds are still quite high that a child of yours will *not* have schizophrenia. The rate of schizophrenia is about 1 percent in the general population. If you have schizophrenia, the odds that your child will have schizophrenia are about 16 percent. So if you have schizophrenia, the chances are more than 8 in 10 that your child will *not* have schizophrenia.

SOME IMPORTANT LEGAL ISSUES: INVOLUNTARY TREATMENT AND GUARDIANSHIP

The Civil Commitment Process

Unfortunately, it often happens that people with schizophrenia fail to take care of their illness. Some flatly refuse to take care of it because they refuse to accept their illness, so the illness has more or less taken over their life. In such cases, the person can reach the point that he or she is no longer capable of making a rational decision about seeking treatment. This can be an extremely trying time for family and friends. They may see a loved one struggling terribly while actively avoidant of getting the help that is needed. Understandably, family members may want the patient to be forced to accept treatment. However, to deprive a person of their freedom (by being hospitalized or treated against their will), an order by a civil court is necessary. Every state has laws that specifically define the circumstances under which involuntary treatment can be used, the specific procedures to be taken to get an order from the court, as well as the limits of the involuntary treatment that can be imposed on a person. Families often find this process very frustrating. It is clear to them (and often providers as well) that the person is in serious need of treatment and will not accept it voluntarily. They do not want their loved one living on the street or placing themselves in dangerous situations because of their impaired judgment. But unless certain conditions are met, a court will not order or require treatment to be imposed against the wishes of any individual. These protections are in place to protect a person's rights to liberty and due process. In years past, it was far too easy to involuntarily place someone into a locked facility based solely on the opinion of a spouse, parent, or doctor. Some would say the pendulum has now swung a little too far in the direction of protecting individual rights. Regardless, we all need to work with the legal system that is in place.

I am most familiar with the civil commitment law in Wisconsin, although laws are somewhat similar across states. The civil commitment law in Wisconsin dictates that three basic standards must be met: (1) the person must have a mental illness (such as schizophrenia, bipolar disorder, or depression), which is formally diagnosed by a physician, psychiatrist, or licensed psychologist; (2) this condition can be effectively treated; *and* (3) the person is *imminently dangerous to himself/ herself or others*. This last standard is the one that creates the most frustration for families and providers. The court will not deprive someone of their liberty—that is, impose involuntary treatment—unless that person poses an *immediate danger*. This means that it must be clear that someone will be hurt *right now* if the patient is not treated. In order to be considered dangerous under this standard, they must have actually tried to hurt someone or themselves or made a realistic threat to do so. Another way to be a danger to oneself is to so seriously neglect one's self-care that there is danger, *right now*, of illness or death. An example would be a diabetic who, because of his/her schizophrenia, decided to stop taking his/her insulin or has stopped eating. Another might be misuse or confusion in the use of prescribed medications where there is a very high chance of accidental overdose. Further, this dangerous behavior must have happened *very recently*, such as within the last one or two weeks. The fact that they may have done something very serious a year or even a month ago does not count in this legal process. Lastly, someone must have *witnessed* this dangerous behavior and be willing and able to testify in court. Without such in-person testimony to the court, the case will be dismissed, no matter how serious the allegations. Unfortunately, I have seen many cases dismissed for this reason.

In Wisconsin, there are basically three ways that a person can be held in a mental health hospital involuntarily. (Again, most states have similar versions of these three methods.) The most common is called an Emergency Detention. A law enforcement officer, police or sheriff, can take someone involuntarily to an authorized mental health facility if they believe the person to be mentally ill and dangerous. They then complete a brief report specifying the facts of the case, most importantly the time that the person was detained and the specific behaviors they believe to be dangerous. This report must also contain the names of eye witnesses who have personally observed this dangerous behavior. If the dangerous behavior is the patient's statement that they will harm themselves or someone else, there still needs to be a witness that observed or heard the patient say this. Again, this dangerous behavior must be recent. All elements must be present in the report, otherwise the case will be dismissed at the Probable Cause Hearing. Unfortunately, many a case has been dismissed because some element of the police report was not completed. A second way someone can be admitted involuntarily is through a Three Party Petition. In this case, three adult citizens can file a statement with the County Corporation Counsel claiming that the patient is mentally ill and dangerous. As above, the dangerous behavior must be recent and at least one of the three petitioners must have observed the dangerous behavior. Once filed, the police will be notified and the person will be detained and brought to the hospital. The last method of involuntary hospitalization is the Treatment Director's Affidavit (TDA). If a patient has come to the Emergency Room or admission center voluntarily, but then decides to leave, the physician or psychologist can file a TDA to keep the patient in the hospital if it is believed that they are mentally ill and dangerous. As with the Emergency Detention, the doctor must clearly state the dangerous behavior, and identify a witness who observed the dangerous behavior. (There is a fourth route to involuntary treatment in Wisconsin, often referred to as the "Fifth Standard." This provides a path to involuntary treatment *before* the person becomes dangerous. However, most professionals and attorneys see this provision as fairly ineffective and very difficult to prove, so it is rarely used. For that reason, I will not describe it further.)

While a person can be held involuntarily in a hospital for seventy-two hours, there must be a Probable Cause hearing within this time frame, otherwise the person must be released. During these seventy-two hours, the person has the right to refuse to take prescribed antipsychotic medication. Note that the Probable Cause hearing is held within three *business days* before a judge or court commissioner. This means that weekends and holidays do not count as any part of the seventy-two hours. This hearing will result in a decision as to whether the above standards have "probably" been met so that the person can continue to be held involuntarily. In order for the court to find probable cause to hold the person, at least one witness who observed the dangerous behavior and a doctor (psychologist or physician) must both testify in person. The doctor is there to testify that they evaluated the patient and that the patient has a treatable mental disorder. If either witness does not appear, the case is dismissed, and the person must be released from the hospital. If the patient is refusing to take prescribed medication, a court order can be obtained at this point to allow medication to be given involuntarily. If probable cause is found, a Final hearing is scheduled, usually within two weeks. The same evidence, as well as any new evidence, is heard in regard to the three standards. If the judge is convinced, with a high level of certainty (more so than at the Probable Cause hearing), the patient can be committed to treatment for an initial period of six months. (If the patient continues to require involuntary treatment, later hearings can extend the commitment for a year at a time.) Court-ordered treatment does not necessarily have to be in a hospital, but can also be applied to outpatient care. It is important to note that the patient is always represented by an attorney during this process. The job of the defense attorney is to prove that the patient *does not need* involuntary treatment or at least to argue for the shortest possible period of commitment. This is an important part of the adversarial component of our nation's legal process, the right to defense counsel, although it is often hard for those outside of the legal system to understand. It is also important to note that there are a few points in this process at which the patient can opt to agree to treatment on a voluntary basis rather than continue with the court proceedings. Signing in voluntarily to a hospital or an outpatient treatment program also means that you can *sign out* whenever you wish.

Guardianship

There are times when a person becomes so severely affected by their illness that they can no longer make good decisions for themselves. This would include financial matters like managing their money and paying bills, medical decisions, and decisions about property. Further, if it also appears extremely likely that the person will *never* regain the ability to make these decisions for himself/herself, a court can appoint a "guardian". The job of a guardian is to make decisions on behalf of the person who has become permanently incapacitated. In order for the court to appoint a guardian, three standards must be proven to a judge: (1) the person has been found "incompetent" to care for himself/herself or manage their own affairs, (2) the condition causing the incapacity is a mental illness (such as schizophrenia) or a mental "defect" (meaning brain injury or brain disorder such as dementia or mental retardation), and (3) this condition is likely to be *permanent* and cannot be effectively treated. This definition is usually applied to conditions like mental retardation, brain injuries, or dementia. Because conditions like schizophrenia can often be improved with treatment, this is usually not seen as grounds for a guardianship. However, there are situations in which the schizophrenia is quite severe and incapacitating, and the illness has proved resistant to treatment (shown no real improvement over several years). In such a case, the condition could be seen as "permanent," and the court may authorize a guardian.

CONCLUSIONS

Knowledge is power. While schizophrenia cannot be cured, the more you know about schizophrenia, the better you will be able to manage it. It is essential that a person who has schizophrenia learns to manage the illness. This is because if you do not manage the schizophrenia, the schizophrenia will manage you. The intent of this book is first to enable and empower the person with schizophrenia to take control of their life rather than allow the schizophrenia to be in control of their life. Secondly, this book is directed toward families and friends who feel left in the dark and want to understand what their loved one is going through and how to help. Lastly, I hope the practical information and perspective of this book will be useful to the many providers who work directly with persons suffering from schizophrenia.

I do hope that the reader has found the information and ideas in this book to be helpful. But this book should not be the educational end point. It is important to keep learning. New medications are in the pipeline. More is being learned about the best way to use the medications, and at the same time, we are developing a greater understanding of their risks.

Psychological techniques continue to be developed to help people with schizophrenia. Maybe most important, patients and families can learn a great deal from each other. Support groups are a great place to get ideas from people who have "been there." Maybe even more gratifying, you may be able to lend hope, help, and support to someone else who is struggling to accept a diagnosis of schizophrenia.

GLOSSARY

affect: Emotional expression. Sometimes people are said to have "flat affect" when they do not seem to express any emotion at all. There are a variety of terms used to describe "affect," as described here.

affective disorder: A disorder involving emotions, emotional expression, or problems controlling emotional expression or intensity.

anhedonia: The inability to experience fun or pleasure.

akathesia: A reversible side effect of some antipsychotic medications, usually seen as a sense of restlessness, pacing, and the feeling that you "can't sit still." When this happens at bedtime, it can make sleep very difficult as well.

antipsychotic medication: A group of medications used specifically to treat mental health conditions like schizophrenia.

auditory: Having to do with sound or hearing.

auditory hallucinations: The experience of hearing voices or sounds that are not actually present.

decanoate: An long-lasting injectable form of a medication.

delusion: This is a fixed belief that something is happening or has happened that quite certainly is not true. Usually, these beliefs sound rather strange and may involve the patient's sense that they are in danger or that they are somehow special.

dystonia: In this book, this refers to a medication side effect that involves stiffness or soreness of muscles, usually in the back and legs. One extreme form is an ocular crisis, in which the muscles that control the movements of the eyes are affected. This condition can be easily and quickly corrected with medication.

euphoria: A state of extreme happiness or pleasure that is completely over-the-top and doesn't fit with what is really happening.

flat affect: Looking monotone, with little or no emotional expression.

hallucination: A perceptual experience that is not real. For example, hearing a voice when there is no one present, seeing an object that no one else can see, or feeling something on your skin when there is nothing there. Hallucinations can occur with any of the senses.

- Auditory—the sense of hearing
- Olfactory—the sense of smell
- Gustatory—the sense of taste
- Tactile—the sense of touch
- Visual—the sense of sight

incongruent affect: The emotional expression doesn't fit with what is happening. For instance, smiling or laughing when talking about something that is actually sad.

labile affect: Emotional expression that is extreme and changes rapidly. For example, happy one moment, crying the next, and then suddenly angry.

metabolic syndrome: A condition that includes obesity, high cholesterol, and high triglycerides, along with elevated blood pressure and elevated blood sugar.

negative symptoms: These are symptoms that indicate the *lack or absence of something* usually present in a healthy person. For instance, the lack of emotional expression, lack of motivation, or the inability to feel pleasure are all considered negative symptoms of schizophrenia.

neuron: A nerve cell.

neuroleptic: A class of medication used to treat symptoms of psychosis.

positive symptoms: Does not mean "good" symptoms. Rather, they are unwanted things that a person does or experiences that are signs or indications of a disorder. Examples are hallucinations, euphoric mood, or depression.

psychosis: A condition in which a person's actions and speech show that they are not perceiving reality correctly. Hallucinations and delusions often are present. Or the person may be so confused or disorganized that they do not have a sense of what is real and what is not. This term describes a condition that could be a result of various factors, such as dementia, street drugs, or schizophrenia.

psychotropic medication: Medication that is prescribed and intended to treat emotional/psychological problems such as depression, anxiety, or schizophrenia.

side effects: The unintended effect of a medication. For instance, a cold medication should help you stop sneezing, but sleepiness may be a side effect.

symptoms: The observable signs of a disorder or condition.

synapse: A tiny gap between the ending of an axon of one neuron and the dendrite of the receiving neuron.

tardive dyskinesia: A side effect that can be caused by antipsychotic medications, although it is quite rare with the newer medications. The problem includes involuntary facial and hand movements. The symptoms are sometimes masked by the medication, so it is not always apparent until the medication is stopped. The condition sometimes goes away, but sometimes it doesn't.

Printed in Great Britain
by Amazon